When Jews and Christians Meet

When Jews and Christians Meet

A Guide for Christian Preaching and Teaching

Clark M. Williamson

CBP Press
St. Louis, Missouri

Library of Congress Cataloging-in-Publication Data

Williamson, Clark M.

When Jews and Christians meet : a guide for Christian preaching and teaching / Clark M. Williamson.

p. cm.

ISBN 0-8272-4224-7 : $9.95

1. Judaism (Christian theology) 2. Christianity and other religions—Judaism. 3. Judaism—Relations—Christianity.

I. Title

BT93.W55 1989 88-27600

261.2′6—dc19 CIP

Printed in the United States of America

Contents

Preface

Three pivotal events drastically affecting Christians in their relationship with Jews have taken place within the lifetimes of many of us. They are the Nazi attempt to see to it that not a single Jew remained alive on planet earth, the establishment of the state of Israel in 1948, and the issuance by the Second Vatican Council of the Roman Catholic Church in 1965 of the *Declaration on the Relationship of the Church to Non-Christian Religions*.

The first has forced many scholars to engage in serious self-criticism of the Christian tradition in the attempt to answer the question: How could this happen in a part of the world that had been Christian for so long?

The second has confronted Christians, for the first time in their history, with the fact of Jewish sovereignty in a Jewish state, something that the Christian tradition had long declared to be contrary to the will of God.

The third recognizes the first two as decisive events happening in the twentieth century and appropriately begins with the words, "In our times . . . ." It affirms that God "does not repent of the gifts He makes nor the calls He issues" to Israel.

The joint impact of these three climactic events has generated an incredible amount of theological scholarship and proposals for new ways to envisage relationships between Christians and Jews. Thinkers have pushed out the frontiers of Christianity, enlarged its horizons, and enabled many Christians to participate in wider and deeper forms of relatedness with Jews. Creative theological work has broken much new ground.

Yet whenever a theological movement exercises great leadership, it faces the risk of running too far ahead of potential followers. Pastors, seminary students, and laity who did not get in the elevator when it was on the ground floor, perhaps because they were studying high school geometry rather than theology at the time, may not yet be able to appreciate the view available when the elevator has reached the penthouse. There is a need, periodically, for a ground floor book, one that opens the door to an exciting ride. This is intended to be such a book.

It is dedicated to Marion Unger and Abraham Unger, M.D., who have played a very important role in my life, being the parents of Barbara, my wife. Not only have they been willing to accept a theologian into the family, but they know what this book is all about without having read it.

1

Grace and Torah

Dealing with the "Old Testament"

In churches today, the "Old Testament" receives both too little attention and the wrong kind of attention. This chapter will seek to show its readers several things: why the "Old Testament" should be the subject of much more Christian preaching and teaching than it is, why the name "Old Testament" is itself open to question, how the "Old Testament" should not be interpreted, and how it should be interpreted. Along the way, we will gain greater awareness of how the Christian faith is enhanced by a fuller appropriation of the faith of Israel. And we will find a greater appreciation of the ongoing faith of Jews who, with Christians, also wait for the coming reign of God, which is ahead for both of us.

Preaching from the "Old Testament"

James A. Sanders, Professor of Old Testament at the School of Theology at Claremont, has criticized the way lectionaries are organized and has proposed a constructive alternative. Because his views are pertinent to the concerns of this chapter, they will be summarized here.

In some congregations, particularly those standing in the various "free-church" traditions, a lectionary is not used. The portions of scripture read and preached on in these congregations depend on the choice and taste of the pastor. Should such a congregation decide to start using a lectionary, that would be a great gain. One reading from the "Old Testament" would be heard every week, and it might occasionally be the text for a sermon. The lectionary makes it possible for preachers to deal with passages of scripture with which they are not familiar or which are not their favorites. Lectionaries enable us to deal with more of the Bible and to relate its readings to the liturgical year.

In spite of these advantages, any lectionary has its limits. There are at least five such limits. The first is that the canon (all the books of the Bible) "is cut up into bits and pieces to serve the calendar" (James Sanders: 258). The Christian year begins in Advent and moves through Christmastide, Epiphany, Lent, Eastertide, and Pentecost. It begins with the expectation of the birth of Christ and culminates with the celebration of the resurrection and the establishment of the church. The whole of the "Old Testament" is brought into correlation with this story, which means that most of it is omitted and that those parts of it that are read tend to be seen as "promises" that are "fulfilled" and set aside by the next reading, taken from the "New Testament."

Therefore, the second limit of the lectionary is that in it "the Old Testament is usually gutted and sacrificed on the altar of the Christian need to believe it has superseded Judaism" (James Sanders: 258). Often, lectionary readings seem to be picked in order to show that in the "Old Testament" the glass was only half full, whereas now it is full of the grace and love of God.

The third limit of the lectionary is that it supports a christocentric, rather than a theocentric, interpretation of the Bible. The way lectionaries structure readings from the scriptures tends to perpetuate the inappropriate way in which some Christians understand their faith, that Jesus Christ made salvation possible and that apart from him and hence apart from the church there is no salvation. Hence, the lectionary also distorts the New Testament, whose writers intended to be understood theocentrically, a point to which we will return in the next chapter. The good news begins in Genesis. The Bible does not spin its wheels for the first three-quarters of its length, only to get down to business with the first chapter of Matthew.

Because the "Old Testament" is cut into bits and pieces by the lectionary, Christians are deprived of the knowledge of the scriptures that the writers of the New Testament assumed their readers would have. These writers "rooted everything they reported of what God was doing in Christ and in the early church in their scripture, that is, in the story of what God had done before"

(James Sanders: 258). Everything that took place happened, said Paul, "according to the scriptures" (1 Corinthians 15:3). Every line in the New Testament is ensconced from behind by the faith and literature of Israel and cannot be understood apart from it. When we read the story, we learn that God is the main character in it, that it is God who graciously reveals God's own deepest personal reality to Israel (von Rad: 8-9). If our reading of the New Testament is not adequately instructed by the "Old Testament," we may fail to see that according to it God reveals God's self to us in Christ, that "*all* of what Jesus said and did pointed to God" (James Sanders: 259).

The last limit of the lectionary is that it does not permit the old practice of preaching continuously through a whole book of the Bible. One of the best things preachers can do to break through the limits of the lectionary would be to begin the practice of studying and preaching through a whole biblical book. Doing so would accomplish one purpose of a lectionary, to treat passages one might otherwise miss, but would also see to it that passages are dealt with in context, a concern with which lectionaries interfere.

What we need in our churches is more, and more adequate, preaching from the "Old Testament." Sanders lists the benefits that would result from such preaching (James Sanders: 262-263). It would introduce a theocentric perspective into the churches. It would stress God's activity as Creator of all peoples and as Redeemer in Israel and in Christ. This would counter the Christian leaning to a self-serving reading of the Bible. It would oppose the continuing anti-Judaism of Christianity. The New Testament would be "put . . . back into the Bible." Such preaching would emphasize social ethics and include personal ethics in a more comprehensive outlook. It would see New Testament eschatology in relation to God's creative and re-creative activity. This approach would underline the freedom of God and of God's grace. We would learn that we cannot turn any gift of God's grace into a condition apart from which God is not free to be gracious to whomever God chooses—even Jews and even us. We would learn that God revealed Christ and that it is not the case that Christ is the only one who revealed God.

Whether lectionaries will ever be more adequately organized than they now are is uncertain. However, preachers do not need to wait for that to take place. The period in the church year after Pentecost used to be referred to as "the church's teaching season." This is the appropriate time for preachers to begin a program of more adequate preaching from the "Old Testament" by dealing in depth with whole biblical books.

A Danger in the Name "Old Testament"

The reader will have noticed the unusual practice of placing the name "Old Testament" in quotation marks and may wonder why this is done. An explanation is due. In the tradition of Christian anti-Judaism, the adjective "old" quickly gained a derisive meaning (Williamson, 1982: 89-105). Jews and Judaism were understood to be "old," that is, obsolete, fossilized, senescent. Jews obstinately cling to what is past and gone, study the "Old" Testament, and derive from it the directions by which they live. Being old, they are religiously out of date. They not only missed but rejected the "new" covenant that God made with gentiles. Christianity is everything new and good that Judaism can never be. Judaism is everything bad and old that Christianity has surpassed and transcended.

The early church soon produced a heretic, Marcion (who died about the year 168), who applied this old/new dichotomy to the scriptures themselves. Marcion argued that the God depicted in the "Old Testament" was a God of law, justice, and wrath, whereas in the "New Testament" we have a new and better God, a God of love and grace. Marcion did a new thing: He divided the scriptures into two testaments, old and new, and rejected the "Old Testament," arguing that it should have no authority in the church. He was the first to propose a canon (a list of books) of the "New Testament." His interest in creating the New Testament was in rejecting the "Old Testament." His New Testament consisted of ten of Paul's letters and the Gospel of Luke. He edited Paul and Luke heavily to make them conform to his point of view.

The church did not go along with Marcion's effort to reject the "Old Testament," but we should not allow ourselves to think that its victory over Marcion's anti-Judaism was complete. Marcion's decision to divide the scriptures into two parts, and his names for them, were retained by the church. Ever since, we have had an "Old" and a "New" Testament. The practice of downplaying the role and authority of the "Old Testament" has persisted. In Marcion, the anti-Jewish theory of certain aspects of the early church became incorporated into a practice, and the practice continues to do its destructive work even when the theory has been forgotten. Hence, we have a problem with the very names "Old" and "New" Testament. What are we to call these collections of scripture?

Let us consider several possible answers. First, Jews have their own name for what Christians call the "Old Testament." For them it is made up of three parts: *Torah*, the five books traditionally attributed to Moses; *Neviim*, all the prophetic books plus Joshua, Judges, and the books of Samuel and Kings; and *Khetuvim*, the writings (Psalms, Proverbs, Job, Ecclesiastes, Song of Songs, Ruth, Esther). From the first letter of each part, T, N, and K, they derive an acrostic, *Tanach*, which is the name for the whole Hebrew Bible. No one suggests that Christians adopt the term *Tanach* for the "Old Testament" or that we refer to scripture readings as drawn from, for example the *Neviim*. We would benefit, however, from knowing more than we do about the tradition of rabbinic interpretation (*midrash*) of the *Tanach* and from hearing good rabbinic preaching from the *Torah* and *Neviim*.

Paul M. van Buren suggests that instead of the terms "Old" and "New Testament," we speak of the Hebrew Scriptures and the Apostolic Writings (van Buren: 122ff). Some seminaries and divinity schools have, in effect, adopted at least the first half of his suggestion, referring in their catalogs to the "Hebrew Bible" rather than to the "Old Testament." In divinity schools where Jewish scholars teach the Hebrew Bible, "Old Testament" is not used. The merit of van Buren's suggestion is that the terms "Old" and "New Testament" do not themselves occur anywhere in the scriptures. Paul the apostle understood himself to be writing letters, not the "New Testament." Further, his letters show that he was interpreting what he called "the scriptures" in the light of his experience of Jesus Christ and that he was interpreting Jesus Christ in the light of the scriptures. He and all the rest of the early church simply called the Hebrew Bible or its Greek translation "the scriptures" (2 Peter 3:16). Van Buren's suggestion, therefore, has the merit of appropriateness; his suggested names "Hebrew Scriptures" and "Apostolic Writings" fittingly refer to the scriptures.

The term "Hebrew Scriptures" is viewed by some as unsatisfactory. The reasons for this seem to be two: First, Christians who do not read Hebrew can hardly claim to be interpreting the Hebrew Scriptures and, second, "Hebrew Scriptures" may not sufficiently state the importance that the "Old Testament" should have in Christian understanding. Hence, one scholar suggests that we use the term "Prime Testament" in place of "Old Testament" (Lacocque: 121). Because the early Christian writings (Paul's letters, the gospels, etc.) were all "occasional, circumstantial writings, not meant for generalized use" (Lacoque: 123), he proposes that the New Testament be regarded as an "appendix" to the Prime Testament (Lacocque: 140). It tells us "what is the living soul" of the word of God that we find in the Prime Testament, but it is in no sense its termination.

Another alternative is to keep the names "Old" and "New Testament," but reinterpret them and explain to our congregations what the terms mean. The fact that the terms "old" and "new" have been misused in the anti-Jewish tradition is not sufficient reason for abandoning them. Just as those of us who believe in the gospel (*evangel*) of Jesus Christ do not have to hand over the word "evangelical" to right-wingers, so those who know how the scriptures speak of things "old" and "new" do not have to abandon these words to those who misuse them.

Whereas the English language has the one word "new," other languages have several words for the different meanings of "new." "New" can mean "brand new" or "renewed." When Jeremiah spoke of "a new covenant" (31:31) that the Lord promised to make with Israel, he used the Hebrew word *chadash*. The Hebrew root for this word usually carries the meaning of "renew" and is used to refer to restoring temples and rebuilding cities, that is, to renewing what is already present. The same word is used in the Hebrew expression "new moon." There is a new moon every month, but it is the same old moon that we newly see. It is not a brand new moon, not a different one from the one last month. Similarly, in the New Testament we have two Greek words for new: *kainos* and *neos*. *Kainos* means "renewed," and *neos* means "wholly new." The writer of Hebrews 8:8-11, referring to the "new covenant," uses the term *kainos*, "renewed."

One option then is to retain the terms "Old" and "New Testament," but to use and explain the word "old" so as to show that we hold dear what is old. Good marriages and good wines show us that some things get better with age. Also, we should explain that we are using the word "new" to mean "renewed."

Each of these alternatives (Hebrew Scriptures and Apostolic Writings, Prime Testament, Old and New Testament reinterpreted) is an appropriate answer to the question of the name. The critical matter for pastors and teachers, whatever set of terms they choose to employ, is to teach why those terms are used and what they mean. Having said all this, we will henceforth remove the quotations marks from the term Old Testament in this book, and we will use all these different names for it.

How Not to Deal with the Old Testament

We began by saying that in our churches we need both more, and more adequate, preaching and teaching from the Old Testament. Before turning our attention to what more adequate preaching and teaching would be, we would do well to indicate the ways in which we should *not* talk about the Prime Testament. Historically, Christians have found many ways to denigrate the God worshiped in the Hebrew Scriptures, the people who worshiped and still worship that God, and the ways in which they did and do worship God. Here we will point out some of the more obvious misinterpretations of the Old Testament.

We should not deal with any passage of the Old Testament in order to show that in it we find only the *type or shadow* of what later becomes *reality or light* in the New Testament. This way of reading the Prime Testament is a proof-texting effort to show that we have a better religion than the Jews had. One way of doing this is to contend that what was revealed to the people of Israel was promises, but only promises, and that these promises have been fulfilled in the New Testament. Those who have only the promises—the Jews—have empty promises. The well of their religion is dry, while ours is full of living water. A more subtle form of this assertion is that Old Testament faith was partially full of the real thing, but that "now" it has been filled full. This way of interpreting the scriptures of Israel denies the freedom of God to be gracious to Israel and works-righteously implies that by doing the good work of becoming Christian, Jews can gain access to God's grace. It empties the Old Testament of religious significance and pours its content into the New Testament, thus denying to continuing Israel its religious legitimacy.

Another standard Christian method of misinterpreting the Prime Testament is *to split the promises and the judgments* of God from one another. This approach applies the judgments of God for idolatry and misbehavior to Israel and applies the promises of God's grace and love to the church. Hence, Jews today stand under God's judgment, but we stand under God's grace. We receive forgiveness and affirmation; they get wrath and rejection. The results of this have been disastrous for Jews and, in different ways, for Christians. For Jews, it has meant that they are pictured as the very essence of evil. How else can God's wrath against them be explained? History shows that that those who are constantly depicted as evil will be made to suffer for the way in which they are caricatured. For Christians it has meant that the prophetic capacity for self-criticism, for criticism of the church on the part of those who love it, is extremely difficult to accept. After all, is not the church perfect? Don't the promises apply to us, the judgments to "them"?

We may not so deal with the Old Testament as *to alienate law and grace from one another*. Christians have too often treated the commandments as the very antithesis of the gracious love of God. They are presented as a burden too heavy to bear, whose only function is to lead us to see the futility of trying to live by them. Characteristically, Jews are spoken of as either works-righteous and boasting because they keep the law or as hypocrites because they do not. Either way, they lose. We, meanwhile, do not have to attend to such "legalistic" matters because the grace of God is available to us. The problem with this way of treating the Prime Testament is that by denying the relation between God's grace and God's justice, it presents a cheap-grace version of Christian faith and claims that this is superior to works-righteous, hypocritical Judaism. If this approach accurately describes Judaism and Christianity, there is not much to choose between them. The good news is that it is not an accurate description. Hence, this is another approach to interpretation that we should avoid.

Another false dichotomy that we should avoid in preaching from the Prime Testament is that of *letter and spirit*. As Christianity developed, it took over a Platonic dualism between letter and spirit and used it to redefine itself over against the "old" law and covenant. On this view, Judaism is entirely concerned with the externalities and superficialities of faith. It is fleshly and carnal. Christianity has to do with the spirit and grace. This is merely another form of the argument that Christianity is a religion superior to Judaism. This argument is not only works-righteous. It is also false. It overlooks the obvious fact that the question of the relation of letter and spirit is a problem within Christianity, as is amply testified by the sheer volume of Christian literalism present to some extent in all churches and profusely in the messages of many television preachers.

The truth is that both Judaism and Christianity and, for that matter, all religions, are complex embodiments of letter and spirit, externality and internality. Christianity without letter, externality, and embodiment would be ghostly and unrecognizable. The inner meaning is what, of course, is important, but every expression of this meaning is an embodiment of it, sometimes in scripture, sermon, book, creed, prayer, liturgy, social action, or in organizational structures: congregations, synods, dioceses, regions. We should neither denigrate embodiment and letter—the only ways in which meaning can be expressed—nor idolize them. Nor should we forget that Judaism is as much spirit as Christianity is letter.

In summary, we should not treat the Hebrew Scriptures in any way that suggests Christianity has *superseded or displaced* Jews and Judaism in the covenant with God, in God's love or favor. "Supersede" is derived from two latin words, *super* (on or upon) and *sedere* (to sit). It refers to the act in which one person takes a seat that has been vacated by another, thus preventing that person from sitting there again. All the ways in which we should not deal with the Old Testament are ways of claiming that Christianity has superseded, taken the place of, Judaism and the Jewish people in God's grace. They all add up to the same result, regardless of whether we claim that we have the reality of which they merely have the shadowy type, or that we receive the promises whereas they receive only condemnation, or that ours is a religion of grace and love in contrast to their legalism and works-righteousness, or that ours is a warm, inward religion of spirit as over against their cold, dry, and legalistic concern with letter and externalities.

Any suggestion that the Prime Testament is the text of a

religion of oldness and the past, whereas ours is one of novelty and vigor, that the particularist, blind, and obdurate Jews have been displaced in God's favor by the new, universal, gentile, and faithful church is a form of "boasting" and works-righteousness that denies the very gospel given us to proclaim. In none of these ways does the gospel of the love of God freely offered to each and all and the command of God that justice be done to each and all permit us to deal with the Prime Testament. Nor are we morally free to claim or imply that Jews are religiously out of business, that they could see (if they were not blind) that Christianity has transcended and overcome Judaism and that therefore they should become Christians. This is to imply, if not to state, that Jews have no right to exist as Jews. One cannot imply this and, at the same time, teach respect for one's neighbors.

How to Deal with the Prime Testament

We will take our cues as to how to interpret the Prime Testament from several contemporary biblical scholars, Jewish and Christian, whose views on the way to understand the Hebrew Scriptures are remarkably compatible. They make it plain that in the Old Testament God is not understood as an unmoved philosophical principle, or a ruthless moral energy, or a despotic Caesar. Rather, God is that boundless love or unconditional faithfulness who is the ground and end of everything that is. This boundless love is disclosed in the Prime Testament to be the Holy One of Israel, the God whose command is based upon the covenant that God made with God's people, and whose covenant with them rests, in turn, upon God's free election of them, upon God's having chosen the patriarchs and having liberated the people from slavery in Egypt and having led them through the wilderness to Sinai. God's covenant and God's commandments expressing God's demand for justice are anchored in God's gracious deeds in history. The *Torah* (instruction, teaching, law) both arises from God's grace and expresses God's grace. Because the relation between grace and *Torah* is the key to a correct understanding of the Prime Testament, we will take it as the theme of the rest of this chapter.

Grace and Torah

God's giving of the ten commandments to Israel at Sinai is prefaced with these words: "I am the Lord your God, who brought you out of the land of Egypt, out of the house of bondage" (Exodus 20:2). "The God who speaks here is the God of grace" (von Rad: 29). This statement succinctly summarizes the first nineteen chapters of Exodus, all of which is prologue to the giving of the *Torah* to Moses. The prologue functions to base Israel's obligations to God on God's gracious deeds on behalf of Israel (Levenson: 37). Israel is to affirm God's rule over Israel by observing the commandments (*mitsvot*) of God. Prior to telling the story of the giving of the *Torah*, Israel recites the history of God's gracious acts on its behalf so that keeping the commandments will be understood as Israel's response to God's unmerited good pleasure. Hence, observing the *Torah* is the means of an intimate and loving relationship with God, of "communion with a loving and personal God" (Levenson: 50).

Israel's very existence as a distinct people, as Israel's faith would have it, depends not upon the merits of Israel, its strength or numbers or any noteworthy qualities, but on an affair of the heart, a love. "Behold," says the Deuteronomist, "to the Lord your God belong heaven and the heaven of heavens, the earth with all that is in it; yet the Lord set his heart in love upon your fathers and chose their descendants after them, you above all peoples, as at this day" (Deuteronomy 10:14-15). Therefore, as the same context makes clear, Israel is to love God, walk in God's ways, and keep God's commandments (Deuteronomy 10:12-13). At the heart of Israel's covenant with God we find a mutual love, the unmerited love of God for Israel and the love of Israel for God (Levenson: 77). Israel loves God by walking in God's way, by keeping God's commandments. God's law is born in love; God's love is given voice in law.

Here we see the essential structure of the biblical faith, which will be repeated in the New Testament. It is not a circle with one center but an ellipse with two foci: the love of God freely offered to each and all and the command of God that justice be done to each and all. The commandments (*Torah*, law) are not external and arbitrary impositions but a form for expressing gratitude and themselves a form of grace.

The word *Torah* is inadequately translated by "law." It means teaching or instruction, the principles or guidelines by which Israel is to walk in the way of God. The Ten Commandments might perhaps better be called the ten "words." It is interesting that they are stated in the indicative, with no hint of reward or punishment connected with them. "You shall not kill." The people of God do not kill. God's will is that they do not. God's people are to be a witness people, witnessing by the way they live to the love and justice of God. The broadest meaning of the term *Torah* is instruction in God's gracious will for a people who accept God's gift of grace. In the whole range of meanings that the word "law" (*Torah*) has in the Old Testament, it is totally comparable to what Christians mean by "gospel" (Hummel: 16).

Orthodox rabbis, studying the *Torah* (here in the sense of the first five books of the Prime Testament), concluded that in it are 613 commandments. This is a long way from the first ten! The totality of commandments was the further development and application of the fundamental guidelines to concrete and particular situations (Myers: 17). For example, because we are to love our neighbors as ourselves (Leviticus 19:18), we are to pay wages to hired workers when the wages are due, and not later (Leviticus 19:13). For the same reason we are not to "curse the deaf or put a stumbling block before the blind" (Leviticus 19:14). Many Christian institutions in recent years have removed architectural barriers to the handicapped from their buildings, perhaps unwittingly applying Leviticus 19:14 to new situations.

The extreme variety of biblical commandments is likely to be confusing to many Christians. We can understand this variety by remembering one principle: that God is sovereign over every aspect of life (von Rad: 49). Therefore, justice is never to be perverted either for the rich or for the poor, who with the stranger are particularly to be loved and dealt with justly. Numerous laws seek to ease the lot of the poor and protect them from extortion. Every seventh year is to be observed as a sabbath (a rest) for the land itself, in which fields are not sown nor vineyards pruned. In order to prevent extreme economic disparity from making the lot of the poor even worse, land was not to be sold in perpetuity. Instead, every seventh year lots were to be cast to determine occupation of the land, and all debts were to be cancelled, a remarkable program of social justice (See Leviticus 25, which contains many laws relating to the sabbath or Jubilee year).

Greater acquaintance with the scope of the *Torah* (teaching, law) as expressive of God's care for all would be of great benefit to Christians as we seek insight into how to deal with the problems of our time. Rather than blame the ecological crisis on the Prime Testament (cf. Genesis 1:28), we could learn from it about how to curb our destructive practices. Deuteronomy 22:6-7 shows that we can destroy a species of bird if we consistently take both the mother and her eggs for food; hence, "you shall let the mother go."

Were an ox or an ass to be yoked together to plow, they would only hurt each other, because they pull at different speeds. So, we do not do this (Deuteronomy 22:10). Nor may we be cruel to animals: "You shall not muzzle an ox when it treads out the grain" (Deuteronomy 25:4). Even building codes fall within the scope of God's concern: "When you build a new house, you shall make a parapet for your roof, that you may not bring the guilt of blood upon your house, if any one fall from it" (Deuteronomy 22:8). Because we are to love our neighbors and because we are not to kill, our buildings must be safe. Nor in our buying and selling may we cheat one another by using an inaccurate system of weights and measures (Deuteronomy 25: 13-15). These few examples will suffice to show that the law reveals the all-inclusiveness of God's love.

In the prophets, the same relation pertains between the gracious love of God and the dual commandment of the love of God and of the neighbor. Although the religion of Israel was patriarchal (yet no more so than that of the church), it rarely uses the term "father" to refer to God, doubtless because of connections this term had with the fertility cult of Baal. Nevertheless, the language of intimate, tender, parental love of God for Israel as God's beloved son was employed (Exodus 4:22-23). Images of Israel as God's child or son, of God and Israel as bride and bridegroom, and motherly images of God's tenderness all express the love of God for Israel. Hosea speaks of God as having loved Israel as a child, having taught Ephraim to walk, having bent down and fed God's children (Hosea 11:3-4). The basic experience of the prophets was an awareness of the pathos of God with Israel, a feeling of the heart of God as well as a hearing of God's voice. (Heschel: 1962, 25-26). Because they had this experience, they too taught *Torah* to the people, "the instruction (*Torah*) of the Lord" (Isaiah 30:9).

Because the scope and depth of God's empathy is so great, God is a God of forgiveness. God's steadfast love or grace (*hesed*) manifest in mercy is a staple of Israelite faith, a point that Christians often fail, perhaps deliberately, to see. God's "righteousness" in the Prime Testament refers to the reliability or steadfastness or loyalty of God's love and grace (Holmgren: 48). The Psalms frequently witness to a God who graciously forgives those who turn to God in repentance: "Have mercy on me, O God, according to thy steadfast love; according to thy abundant mercy, blot out my transgressions" (Psalm 51:1). While Israel was yet a sinner, God saved it from Egypt (Psalm 106). When the Old Testament talks of the righteousness of God, we should not make the mistake of thinking that this God is stern and judgmental. In Jewish thought, God's righteousness is a way of talking of the dependability of God's love and the readiness of God to forgive. The sacrificial rituals and the Day of Atonement were means of grace by which God's forgiveness was made available (Klassen: 73ff.).

Another way in which Israel understood the grace of God entailed the view that this grace was by no means merely for Israel. The people of Israel was to be a priestly people, to serve others, not themselves. God's covenant with Israel was not fundamentally for Israel's own good but for that of all human beings, gentiles as well as Jews. Israel is chosen as an instrument that God can use so that all peoples may come to know God and God's purposes for them. God's initial promise to Abraham was that "by you all the families of the earth shall bless themselves" (Genesis 12:3). Isaiah taught that this promise would come about when Israel would teach Assyria and Egypt to worship God (Isaiah 19:23-25). The writer known as Second Isaiah, who lived in exile in Babylonia, interpreted God's purpose in sending Israel into exile as a missionary one: "I have given you as a . . . light to the nations, to open the eyes that are blind" (Isaiah 42:6-7). Israel's Babylonian neighbors will begin to say, "'I am the Lord's,' another will call himself by the name of Jacob" (Isaiah 44:5). The grace of God was not exclusive to Israel:

> It is too light a thing that you should be my servant
> to raise up the tribes of Jacob
> and to restore the preserved of Israel;
> I will give you as a light to the nations.
> That my salvation may reach to the end of the earth.
> (Isaiah 49:6)

The purpose of the Book of Jonah, from which the story of the big fish is not to distract us, is to remind Israel of her responsibility to Nineveh, one of the more significant centers of gentile culture (Knight: 27). Later, the Jewish tradition would develop further its understanding of the vocation of the Jewish people to serve as a source of light for all the world (Bokser: 90).

Conclusion

What we learn from this all too brief look at the Prime Testament is the radical monotheism that is as basic to the faith of Christians as it is to that of Jews. This monotheism gives voice to the faithfulness of God, which demands our faithfulness in response. For Christians as for Jews, the mystery that enfolds and embraces our life is none other than the covenant God of Israel who reveals Godself to us in the story of Israel, in the law and the prophets, to be the God of an unparalleled promise and command.

The promise is the absolutely free and loving offer, no strings attached, of the grace of God as the only authentic way in which we can understand ourselves and our neighbors. God's command is that we understand ourselves in trust and faithfulness, in terms of God's grace alone, thereby being freed to fulfill the law, which is summarized in two commandments: "You shall love the Lord your God with all your heart, and with all your soul, and with all your might," and "You shall love your neighbor as yourself" (Deuteronomy 6:5; Leviticus 19:18; cf. Mark 12:30-31).

If we understand the faith of Israel, we will understand the faith of Jesus and Paul. If we preach from the Prime Testament in the light of what it has to teach us, we will keep the commandment to love our neighbors as ourselves by teaching respect for them.

2

Jesus and Paul in Context

Outdated Assumptions

A major barrier to teaching respect for Jews and Judaism is found in the assumptions even well-intentioned readers often bring to the New Testament. These assumptions have to do with what Jewish faith in the first century was like, and how Jesus and Paul are to be understood in relation to the Judaism of their times. As a rule, we tend to "know" that Judaism was an inauthentic faith and that the significance of Jesus and Paul is that they liberated their followers from a bad and oppressive religion. It is bad enough that this view communicates falsehoods about Judaism, and worse that it trivializes Jesus and Paul.

The distorting character of modern interpretations of Judaism was pointed out almost seventy years ago by George Foot Moore. In a classic article, Moore argued that until the nineteenth century, Christian interest in Judaism was not scholarly but belligerent; it hoped to prove that Jesus fulfilled and negated Judaism. In spite of the fact that the intent of nineteenth century writers was scholarly, they used the views of Judaism that they had inherited from their forebears, while failing to pay enough attention to the fact that these views had been gathered "from every conceivable motive *except* to serve as material for the historian" (Moore: 221). This is the last thing a scholar should do to gain a fair idea of what faith meant to its adherents.

Moore isolated several themes that characterized this modern and biased view of Judaism: (1) that it was a religion *based on* legalism; (2) that it denied the grace of God; (3) that it believed our relation to God to be based on the balance between our merits and demerits; (4) that it was uncertain about salvation, anxious about not having done enough good works, and self-righteously feeling it had accomplished much; and (5) that for Judaism God was remote from people, withdrawn, and unavailable. Moore severely criticized this interpretation of Judaism as one-sided in its use of Jewish sources, as using Jewish sources only as a foil for the self-validation of Christianity, and as belittling everything Jewish and aggrandizing everything Christian (Moore: 242).

In spite of Moore's work, the tendency to belittle everything Jewish and aggrandize everything Christian continued to persist in Christian writing on the New Testament period, thus necessitating a new criticism of it. Recently, therefore, Christian scholars have taken up Moore's concern anew, seeking to expose the bias in many treatments of Judaism and to replace them with more accurate accounts. Their work may be conveniently summarized under four headings: the so-called "late Judaism," law and legalistic piety, the Pharisees, and Jewish responsibility for the crucifixion of Jesus.

"*Late Judaism*," the very name that much modern scholarship uses for the Judaism of the time of Paul and Jesus, is revealing. It is called "late Judaism," as in "the late (that is, dead) Mr. Smith." This is the name given by German writers to the Judaism of the period from the Babylonian exile (597 B.C.E.) to the war with Rome and the destruction of the Temple (66-70 C.E.). Obviously, this name gives voice to a negative evaluation of Judaism. A more descriptive name is "Second Temple Judaism," and that is what scholars increasingly use.

"Late Judaism" is characterized as an absurd result of a decadent, "blind" rabbinic scholarship which is preoccupied with the letter of the law. As such, it is preparatory for, and inferior to, Christianity. In this view, Jesus rejects this "old" Judaism and, with his words and work, no longer forms a part of the history of Israel. In him the history of Israel has come, rather, to its end. What belongs to the history of Israel is the process of his rejection and condemnation by the Jerusalem religious community. Late Judaism was in a state of decadence, orthodoxy, and legalism. Its faith was externalized and rigid; God had become distant and the prophetic message forgotten. Jesus is understood as the decisive rejection of this old, dead Judaism.

Law and legalistic piety, said to be characteristic of "late Judaism," are condemned. Legalistic piety is the "cancer" of Judaism

(Jeremias: 1971: 227), "the piety that separates us from God." Consequently, legalistic exegesis of the "old" Testament is "blind." and only the church can read the scriptures properly, whereas legalistic Jews were deaf to the gospel.

The Pharisees, in the old model, continue to be represented as *the* enemies of Jesus' teaching. When Jon Sobrino discusses Jesus' approach to prayer, he does so under the rubric of "Jesus' Criticism of Contemporary Prayer" (Sobrino: 146). He starts with the parable of the Pharisee and the publican, in which, he says, "Jesus condemns the prayer of the Pharisees [note the plural] because it is the self-assertion of an egotistical 'I' and hence vitiated at its very core" (Sobrino: 147). The Pharisee's "pole of reference" is not God but himself. Also, the Pharisee is "even less oriented to other human beings. He holds them in contempt . . . and he thanks God that he is not like them" (Sobrino: 147). The prayer of the Pharisees is a mechanical ceremony of self-deception.

Jewish guilt in the death of Jesus is widely affirmed on the basis of this set of outdated assumptions: "The crucified Lord is betrayed and abandoned by his friends, rejected by his people, repudiated by the Church of the Old Testament" (Rahner: 237). "It was an act of unparalleled risk which Jesus performed when, from the full power of his consciousness of sovereignty, he openly and fearlessly called these men [the Pharisees] to repentance, and this act brought him to the cross" (Jeremias, 1969: 267).

It is stupefying that such a thoroughly bleak and prejudiced picture of Judaism in the first century could still be drawn by influential scholars, so long after it has been decisively refuted. Nonetheless, it has continued in use and has been sketched here to alert Christian preachers and teachers to it. It can be found in secondhand form in commentaries and theological works and can be transported from there into sermons and class discussion, as long as we fail to be suspicious of it.

More Recent Scholarship

Because many readers of this book are apt to be seminary graduates who may want to catch up on the fresh scholarship that has been done on the Judaism of Jesus' time and to discover the sources by which this book itself is informed, we will here indicate briefly where some of this new scholarship can be found. An excellent bibliography has been compiled by Eugene J. Fisher in an article entitled "The Impact of Christian Jewish Dialogue on Biblical Studies" (Fisher: 1983). Another bibliography of Christian scholarship on the subject and on the reinterpretation of the New Testament in the light of it has been produced by the present author (Williamson: 1987). A sweeping overview and employment of recent scholarship on Judaism is found in the work of Shaye Cohen (Cohen: 1987).

E.P. Sanders' stunning scholarly achievement has shown, without equivocation, that the assumptions held by those who interpret Jesus and Paul as contradicting Judaism are without foundation. Sanders concludes that "the Judaism of before 70 kept grace and works in the right perspective, did not trivialize the commandments of God, and was not especially marked by hypocrisy" (Sanders: 1977: 427). His exhaustive study of the original sources convinces him that the literature of Judaism is as free of the features attributed to it by the "late Judaism" view as it could possibly be (Sanders: 1977: 427). Instead, it kept in a sound relationship the promise and command of God and encouraged humility toward the God who chose and would one day redeem Israel.

Jesus in Context: What Is Not True

When we look afresh at the figure of Jesus in the light of this new scholarship, things look different indeed. Scholars who know the most about the law (*Torah*) in Second Temple Judaism find no significant points of disagreement on it between Jesus and his contemporaries, and truly none that would lead to his death (Sanders, 1985: 55). They further note that if Jesus had opposed the validity of the Mosaic code, it is passing strange that the apostles in Jerusalem were ignorant of this fact (Sanders, 1985: 55-56, 268). These scholars deny that in the time of Jesus the Pharisees controlled Judaism, that ordinary people (the *'amme ha-arets*) were regarded by the Pharisees as sinners, that the leaders of Judaism (the Pharisees) excluded and oppressed the ordinary people, that Jesus differed from the Pharisees by offering forgiveness to repentant sinners, that Jesus offended the Pharisees by associating with common folk, and that Jesus' behavior accounted for his crucifixion. All this is out the door.

The purity laws were not oppressive of ordinary people, nor were they required to avoid impurity. Such laws had to do only with what one must do, after contacting impurity, before entering the temple. Luke describes Mary and Joseph as observing the purity laws pertaining to childbirth (Luke 2:22-24). Normal human relations were not affected by the purity laws and most impurities were "cleansed" by the immersion pool and by waiting for the sun to set. No prescriptions in the purity law can take precedence over the commandment to love one's neighbor, including the laws pertaining to hand washing, the only purity law discussed in the gospels.

The old view of Judaism as excessively legalistic held that Jesus was distinctive because he held out to ordinary people the offer of forgiveness of sins. This contradicts one feature of Judaism about which everybody should be informed, the "view that forgiveness is *always* available to those who return to the way of the Lord" (Sanders, 1985: 202). The truth is that Jews think Christians make forgiveness too complicated a matter. Any Jew in Jesus' day who desired God's forgiveness could have gotten a quick answer from any religious leader, whether priest or Pharisee: God's arms are always open to any sinner who repents and turns to God. The notion that the Pharisees were offended by Jesus' openness to repentant sinners is absurd (Sanders, 1985: 204). Only the Romans would have objected to the conversion of tax collectors.

A growing number of scholars doubt that there were any important points of disagreement between Jesus and the Pharisees. Before the destruction of the temple in 70 C.E., the Pharisees hardly left Jerusalem and there would probably have been none in Galilee in Jesus' time. It is unrealistic to think that "the Pharisees" trooped about the countryside to inspect the hands of Jesus' disciples, to see if they had been washing, which was in any case not a requirement for lay people, which the disciples were. The "conflict stories" involving Jesus and the Pharisees "were composed [later] in the light of debates between Christianity and Judaism" (Sanders, 1985: 265).

In short, the picture of Jesus that sets up an opposition between him and Judaism has fallen to pieces. It is not conceivably the case that Jewish leaders would have been offended by the fact that some people were repenting of their sins. Nor is it conceivable that Jesus would have been charged with blasphemy because he spoke for God. There was no prohibition on speaking for God, and prophets managed to do it for a considerable period without ever being charged with blasphemy. So, there was no important dispute about the law nor significant conflict with the Pharisees.

Jesus in Context: What Might Be True

What can we say, positively, and within the bounds of historical possibility, that is true of Jesus of Nazareth? We must recognize the difficulty of working backwards from late first-century sources (the gospels); we must note that everything in them is there for a theological purpose, not as a matter of historical reminiscence. Nonetheless, we can make some statements about Jesus that it is more reasonable to accept than to deny.

First, we ought to get his name straight. "Jesus" is a gentile name, what we get when we transliterate from Hebrew or Aramaic into Greek, and then from Greek into English. Were we to transliterate directly from Hebrew to English, it would come out "Joshua." Were we to move directly from Aramaic to English, it would come out "Yeshua." A Hebrew or Aramaic name is a short sentence. Joshua or Yeshua means "Yahweh is salvation." Every time we Christians say or sing that "at the name Jesus every knee shall bow" we are saying that "at the name of 'Yahweh is salvation' every knee shall bow." We do not always have to say "Joshua" instead of "Jesus," but sometimes we should, just to remind ourselves who he is.

Second, the land of Israel (the *eretz Yisrael*) is a principal character in the story of Jesus. He cannot be understood apart from it. Luke preserves traditions indicating that shortly after birth Jesus became a "son of the covenant" and at adolescence what would much later be called a "son of the commandment" (*bar mitzvah*). Since the land of Israel was part of the covenant promise, Jesus was attached to this land through the structure of his own experience and the bonds of faith. He was baptized in the Jordan river, roamed the Judean wilderness, made the Passover pilgrimage to Jerusalem, and was executed by Pontius Pilate on the Hill of the Skull.

Third, Jesus was more specifically a Galilean, a northern, non-Judean Jew, yet a Jew committed, probably exclusively, to his fellow Jews: "I was sent only to the lost sheep of the house of Israel" (Matthew 15:24). When he sent out his disciples, he charged them: "Go nowhere among the Gentiles, and enter no town of the Samaritans, but go rather to the lost sheep of the house of Israel" (Matthew 10:5-6). The mission to the gentiles was the work of the later church, following prophets of their own time whom they believed spoke for the risen, living Jesus. He fits well into the mold of the northern prophets, Elijah and Elisha. A bond of sympathy may have existed between women and Jesus, similar to that found between women and Elijah and Elisha.

Fourth, Jesus was a wandering teacher, committed to the renewal of Jewish life under the *Torah*. In Mark's gospel, beneath the picture of Pharisaical hostility to Jesus, we see the Pharisees pictured as concerned to come to terms with Jesus. They state the criteria of a good teacher: a good teacher courts no one's favor, does not tamper with the truth in order to be liked, and teaches the way of God in truth (Mark 12:14). Then they give Jesus a theological text, which is probing—the question about taxes to Caesar. The taxes are merely illustrative, not the point, which is that Jesus is a teacher in Israel and as such the Pharisees want to test him, which is entirely proper. Equally so is his willingness to be tested. Colleagues are supposed to take one another seriously in just this way. Among the Aramaic words in the gospels is the title *rabbi* or *rabboni*, Aramaic for "teacher." Jesus seems to have been so addressed by his followers.

Jesus' teachings seem to have taken a form very close to that of the contemporary school of Hillel, perhaps slightly more radical than the Hillel school. His method of teaching, "You have heard it said, but I say unto you," is quite similar to the Pharisaic method: "You have read, but the meaning is." This is the method of "oral *Torah*," by which the meaning of the written *Torah* was changed to meet changing circumstances, to make the burden of the Law easy and its yoke light. Such proclamations as "the Sabbath was made for man, not man for the Sabbath" (Mark 2:27) have clear parallels in Hillel: "Scripture says: 'The Sabbath is holy for *you*' (Exodus 31:14). This means it is given to you, not you to the Sabbath" (*Yoma*, 85b). Some of the teachings attributed to Hillel (an older contemporary of Jesus) "are in spirit and even in exact wording close to the teachings of Jesus" (Neusner: 13). Some scholars think that Jesus was more iconoclastic toward outward forms than were Hillel and his followers, but this difference could well be accounted for by the fact that the gospels were written for gentile audiences.

Fifth, Jesus was a *hasid*. This word is related to the noun *hesed*, which means "steadfast love" or "loving kindness." God's *hesed*, God's faithfulness, is a standard Jewish way of talking about what Christians call God's "grace." Typically, a *hasid* would rise above the demands of the law in order to help a person in need. There was no law against doing this, and there were situations, such as saving a life, which required the suspension of all other laws that might conflict with doing so. The *hasidim* (plural) not only did good deeds but deeds of miracle-working power. Galilee had a large number of *hasidim*. Hanina, a disciple of Johanan ben Zakkai (founder of the Pharisaic academy at Jamnia) flourished in Galilee about the time of Jesus. Honi the drawer of circles, like Elijah on Mount Carmel, was said to be able to make it rain.

Jesus' only reported weather miracle was the stilling of the storm (Mark 4:35-41). He did perform a variety of healings and exorcisms. He restored shriveled limbs and lost speech, hearing, and sight. A large aspect of Jesus' activity was the deeds of love and mercy of a *hasid*. Typically he attributed healings not to his own power but to the faith of the person healed: "Your faith has made you well" (Mark 5:34). Christians often think that Jesus got in trouble with Jewish authorities because he healed on the sabbath, thus violating laws against work on the sabbath. But among the clear definitions of what constitutes work on the sabbath, healing is not included.

Sixth, Jesus was a man of prayer and worship. The God whom he called "*Abba*" ("Daddy"), a term of endearment, was the God of Israel. While he sometimes went to a secluded place to pray, he more often went to the synagogue "as his custom was" (Luke 4:16). The prayer he taught his disciples (the Lord's prayer) resonates with the piety of the synagogue and Jewish family. The divine name is holy and not pronounced. God is asked to allow his reign to begin ("thy will be done on earth"), the time when justice and peace shall rule. God is praised as the gracious and nurturing ground of our being ("give us this day our daily bread") and is asked to forgive our sins. Jesus was a man of prayer—Jewish prayer.

Seventh, like the Pharisees and unlike the Sadducees, Jesus believed strongly in the age to come. He was assured that God was faithful to God's word and would see to it that the justice that God had promised would come. A new age of the reign of God would be launched. The parables of the mustard seed and the wheat and the tares, among others, express this eschatological faith. The theme common to these parables is the working out of justice in God's own good time: the fig tree blossoms, the yeast rises, the seed grows, all in due season. God's rule will inevitably come. Jesus apparently thought that this would be "soon," but we must remember that in apocalyptic talk "soon" does not mean in a short time. It expresses the sense that history is in a deep crisis, which it is.

Eighth, Jesus did not proclaim himself as Israel's messiah. Instead, he preached the good news of the coming reign of God. The later church hailed Jesus as the Christ, and thus the proclaimer became the proclaimed. But in his gospel there was no christology. We do not know how Jesus understood himself. Each time the title "Christ" is used in the gospels, it is on the lips of someone else as their confession of faith in him. Later, two things happened. The early church believed in him as the messiah, although not in a simple, straightforward way. He still had to come back and finish the job (Acts 3:17-23). (The messiah was to bring peace and justice to all; if you have looked around lately, you have seen that they have not come.)

Also, as soon as the mission to the gentiles began, new ways of talking about Jesus had to be developed, because "messiah" did not convey any meaning to gentiles. So in Paul, the apostle to the gentiles, there is no sentence that says "Jesus is the Christ." Rather, for Paul "Christ" has become part of a name, Jesus Christ, and other words have to be used to talk of his significance. The term that came to prevail was "Word (*Logos*) of God." We see this also in John's gospel, where the writer has to explain the meaning of the term "messiah" to his readers (1:41). The great creeds of the early church (Nicaea, Chalcedon) do not mention the term "messiah."

Last, Jesus was a storyteller. Among Jews the *mashal* (parable) was a favored way of teaching. Jesus' *mashal* of "a man who had two sons" has been retitled by Christians as "the parable of the prodigal son," perhaps because we like to see ourselves in the prodigal and think the parable is about us. In the text, however, it is announced as a *mashal* about "a man who had two sons." As Luke edited this parable (15:11-24), the prodigal virtually becomes a gentile, and the story has the effect of including gentiles. What Christians usually fail to note about this parable, in which they make the elder brother into the type of "the Jew," is that it is the elder brother's faithfulness to the father that enables the father to be a father, to be there when the younger son returns. Since the father had already divided his living between the two sons, when he presented the prodigal with the fatted calf, the robe, and the ring, he was able to be gracious to him because of the elder brother's faithfulness. Had the elder brother squandered his half of the estate, too, there would have been no home to which the prodigal could return. At the end the father affirms the elder brother: "all that is mine is yours." We cannot overlook the fact that the church rewrote the stories to give them an edge against Jews. Usually, however, by a careful reading we can detect the "seams" in the parable and reinterpret it in the light of Jesus' mission "to all the lost sheep of the house of Israel" (Matthew 10:6).

The Crucifixion of Jesus

If the previous points are probably true about Jesus of Nazareth, readers might well ask, "Why did 'the Jews' crucify him?" The answer is simple: "The Jews" did not crucify him. Here are the reasons for this conclusion. First, at the time of the writing of the gospels (the late first century) the church needed the "benign neglect" of the Roman Empire in order to avoid persecution. To ward off repressive measures, the gospel writers shifted the blame for the persecution of Jesus and Paul from Roman to Jewish opponents. Second, in Jewish and secular historical literature, Pilate comes across as "unbending and recklessly hard," in contrast to the comparatively innocent picture of him in the gospels (Schurer: 198). Tiberius Caesar relieved Pilate of his duties because of the turmoil created by Pilate's slaughter of a group of Samaritans.

Third, the story of the trial of Jesus in Mark (and hence in Matthew and Luke) is motivated not by historical interests but by

Mark's need to support his community in its own trials (Donahue: 211). Fourth, if we read the stories in the four gospels in the order in which they were written, we find that Pilate becomes increasingly innocent and Jews increasingly guilty.

"He was executed by the Romans," concludes E.P. Sanders, "and if Jews had anything to do with it—that is, if he were not executed simply because he caused a public disturbance—the instigators of his death would have been those with access to Pilate. Chief among these were the leaders of the Priesthood" (Sanders, 1985: 293). Yet in a more precise sense the culprit is not "the Romans," either, but "the Roman imperial system" (Rivkin: 117).

The historian Ellis Rivkin helpfully shows us that we put matters wrongly when we ask "who crucified Jesus?" We should ask "what crucified Jesus?" The emperor appointed the procurator. The procurator appointed and controlled the high priest. The high priest convoked his privy council. The empire exacted harsh tribute from the people. The procurators and particularly Pilate drove the people into a frenzy and stirred Judea with violence. The system bred revolutionaries and produced charismatics. The conclusion to which scholarship increasingly points is that merely by attracting a following, any Galilean would come unfavorably to the attention of a nervous and repressive Pilate (Williamson, 1982: 30-46).

Paul in Context: A New Perspective

If we are to teach respect for Jews and Judaism while working with the letters of Paul, we will have to pay attention to our improved understanding of first-century Judaism, which in recent years has led scholars to think radically new thoughts about Paul. The traditional approach to Paul has assumed that Judaism in Paul's time, typified by the Pharisees, was a legalistic and works-righteous faith. It has assumed that Paul, convinced of the bankruptcy of Judaism, set forth his gospel of freedom from the law in conscious opposition to Judaism (Black: 47-48).

Typically, this approach lays great stress on Paul's experience on the Damascus Road, interpreting it as a "conversion" from the bankruptcy of Jewish legalism to the gracious truth in Jesus Christ. Protestant theologians and scholars project their (and

Luther's) difficulties with Christian legalism onto Paul and conclude that, like Luther, Paul was driven to despair by the "intolerable burden" of the law (Tillich: 10-13). In recent years, however, a troubling question has arisen, prompted by our improved understanding of Judaism: What if Paul knew at least as much about Judaism as we do and understood it just as well? If so, he could not have opposed it as he is said to have done. On the other hand, if the received view of his opposition is true, must we not agree with those scholars who say that Paul was fundamentally wrong about Judaism (Schoeps: 213-218)? But if he was wrong, why should we pay attention to him?

Armed with a better understanding of Judaism and questioning the traditional interpretation of Paul as having opposed a Judaism that never existed, several scholars are now establishing a new perspective on Paul. They do not agree on any number of interpretive measures with respect to Paul, but they do agree that a new approach is needed. Here we will take a brief look at several of their contributions. Readers should consult these scholars' works referred to or to the present author's earlier effort at reconsidering Paul (Williamson, 1982: 47-63).

The most consistent attempt to see Paul anew is found in the work of Lloyd Gaston. His method is to confine himself to Paul's own writings, setting to one side Acts and letters attributed to Paul but about which scholars doubt Paul's authorship. He takes as crucial Paul's commissioning as apostle to the gentiles and interprets him as just that. He notes that the term "justification" appears only in contexts where the status of Paul's gentile converts is discussed. Paul's major concern was the legitimacy of the mission to the gentiles: "Is God the God of Jews only? Is he not God of Gentiles also?" (Romans 3:29).

Paul did not undergo a conversion from one religion to another but underwent a significant change in his attitude toward the mission to the gentiles. Paul's only reference to his Damascus experience speaks of God's being "pleased to reveal his Son to me, in order that I might preach him among the Gentiles" (Galatians 1:16). This language is reminiscent of that found in the prophets who received a call to the gentiles (Isaiah 49:1, 6; Jeremiah 1:5). If this was a "conversion," it was like the "conversion" of John Wesley, who did not change his religion but came into truer possession of it.

Central to Gaston's interpretation is Paul's account of the conversation with the pillars of the Jerusalem church (Galatians 2:1-10). The result of this conference was the agreement "that we should go to the Gentiles and they to the circumcised" (2:9). Gaston believes that Paul lived up to this agreement throughout his career, preached strictly to gentiles, and never encouraged Jews to abandon the *Torah*. He offers as evidence that fact that all of Paul's letters are clearly written to gentiles. He writes to those who "turned to God from idols" (1 Thessalonians 1:9), to those who once were Gentiles and "were led astray to dumb idols" (1 Corinthians 12:2), to those who formerly "were in bondage to beings that by nature are no gods" (Galatians 4:8), and speaks of his apostleship as "for bringing about the obedience of the faith for the sake of his name among all the nations, including yourselves" (Romans 1:5-6). Two later letters from Paul's "school" are also to gentiles (Colossians 2:13 and Ephesians 2:11-12). Hence, everything Paul wrote was to gentiles and dealt with gentile problems, chiefly the situation of gentiles in relation to the law (Gaston: 9-11). If Paul has any quarrel with his fellow Jews, it is not about Judaism as such but about the terms on which gentiles are to be admitted into the people of God—with or without circumcision.

Gaston's thesis is that legalism, "the doing of certain works in order to win God's favor and be counted righteous, arose as a gentile problem and was not a Jewish problem at all" (Gaston: 28). It was gentiles not included in the covenant of God's grace who thought that they had to establish their righteousness by certain "works of the law" (which is not a Jewish expression). The content of Paul's gospel is that God will justify the gentiles out of God's faithfulness; hence the importance to Paul of Abraham, to whom the initial promise had been given for "all peoples."

E.P. Sanders agrees that in Paul there is no criticism of Judaism. For him the usual kinds of problems attested by Christian interpreters of Paul result from a misunderstanding both of Judaism and of Paul. Paul is viewed as if he were arguing that we cannot merit salvation by doing enough good deeds and it is thought that Judaism holds such a view, so that Paul's argument is taken to be against Judaism. Not only does careful study of Jewish writings fail to reveal such a position, but that is not Paul's view in any case. Paul's issue is whether his "gentile converts must accept the Jewish law in order to enter the people of God" (Sanders, 1983: 20).

Paul's stance on Judaism, the law, and gentiles, is understood by some scholars today as an effort to provide support for the social reality of sectarian gentile-Christian communities that did not observe the requirements of the *Torah* (Watson). The new perspective notes that in Paul's famous comment about Christ "as the end of the law" (Romans 10:4) the Greek word translated "end" is *telos*. Christ is not the termination of the law but its purpose, in that the law (*Torah*) provided for the inclusion of gentiles within the purposes of God. Throughout his life Paul was no opponent of Judaism but a devout Jew who understood his mission solely as bringing good news to gentiles (Cunningham).

E.P. Sanders interprets Paul with the use of a functional understanding of religious groups. What does one have to do to "get in"? What does one have to do to "stay in"? He sees Paul not as against Judaism but as against Christian missionaries who thought that gentiles must accept the law "*as a condition of* or a basic requirement for membership" (Sanders, 1983: 19) One "gets in" by God's grace, but once in one is then enabled and required to keep all the law, summarized in the commandment to love the neighbor as oneself (Romans 13:8-10; Galatians 5:14). Paul even produces the amazing sentence: "Neither circumcision counts for anything nor uncircumcision, but keeping the commandments of God" (1 Corinthians 7:19). The pattern of religion is the same in Paul and in Judaism: grace and commandment, indicative and imperative. We get in by grace; we stay in by works of love done to the neighbor; "in both rabbinic literature and Paul's letters, remaining in the in-group is conditional on behavior" (Sanders, 1983: 111).

Christology and the Teaching of Respect

We have been at pains to show that Paul's description of himself is true: "circumcised on the eighth day, of the people of Israel, of the tribe of Benjamin, a Hebrew born of Hebrews; as to the law a Pharisee, as to . . . righteousness under the law blameless" (Philippians 3:5-6). Much of this description would apply to Jesus of Nazareth, who was also circumcised on the eighth day, of the people Israel, a Hebrew born of Hebrews, known in his time as *Rabbi Yeshua ha Notsri*, Rabbi Jesus of Nazareth.

We have also tried to show that Jesus and Paul shared the same faith in the God of Israel as the God of a unique promise and a unique command, the promise of the love of God offered freely to each and all and the command of God that justice be done to each and all of those whom God loves. For Jesus the promise of God was directed to all "the lost sheep of the house of Israel" and for Paul it was directed to all the gentiles, in keeping with the promise to Abraham, which included "all the peoples of the earth." Paul saw this promise not fulfilled but *confirmed* (Romans 15:8) in the increasingly successful gentile mission of the early church. The structure of this faith is shared by Paul, Judaism, Jesus, and the Old Testament.

From Paul, we Christians also learn who we are. Ephesians, written by one of Paul's students, puts it rather well. We are gentiles who were "alienated from the commonwealth of Israel, and strangers to the covenants of promise, having no hope and without God in the world" (2:12). Christ did not free us from the *Torah*, because we were not "under" it in the first place. We were strangers to it and to God. We did not know the God of Israel and instead were a-theists, without God. While Jews were learning to live by faith in Yahweh, my Irish ancestors were worshipping Maeve and Fergus, two well-endowed fertility deities, painting their faces blue, and baying at the moon.

Through the church's preaching of Christ, however, we have come to understand who God is, who we are, and what Jesus means to us. God is the God of Israel, the God of a unique promise and a unique command. We are people who can understand ourselves rightly in any ultimate sense in terms of and only in terms of the love of God, which frees us to love our neighbors as ourselves. The meaning of Jesus to us is that it is through him, as proclaimed by the church, that we come to understand ourselves in relation to God in the only way in which we can rightly do so. To have Christ as Lord is the same as having the God of Israel as God. Only through a Jew could this saving knowledge come to us gentiles, because all of us were "without God."

The work of Christ was to make us "fellow citizens with the saints [the Jews] and members of the household of God" (Ephesians 2:19). When we think about christology we should remember that it answers a threefold question: Who is God? Who are we and who am I? What is the meaning of Jesus to us and to me?

Had the church remembered that the one we call "Savior" and "Lord" was *Rabbi Yeshua ha Notsri*, son of Miriam, who died on a Roman gibbet to the sanctification of the divine name, we have to ask whether there would have been so many pogroms, so much hatred of Jews. Would there have been an Auschwitz?

3

The Gospels and Acts

Dealing with the Gospels

When we turn our attention to the New Testament, we find it difficult to teach or preach from it without engaging in the "teaching of contempt" for Jews and Judaism. One reason for this is found in some books of the New Testament, chiefly the gospels and the Book of Acts. We need to learn how to recognize and eliminate the incorrect and negative picture of Jews and Judaism present in parts of the New Testament and in the assumptions that we bring to our reading of it.

The Time of the Gospels

Although the gospels refer constantly to events in the career of Jesus, which took place in the first third of the first century, they come from the last third of the first century, a time drastically different from that about which they speak. Written in Greek, the gospels received their final form between the years 70 and 100 C.E., with Mark being the earliest. Matthew was written between 80 and 90 C.E., Luke-Acts between 85 and 95 C.E., and John about 100 C.E.. Obviously, these dates are not exact; some scholars disagree about them and the order in which the gospels were produced. In order to understand how negative images of Jews and Judaism found their way into the gospels (including the Book of Acts, the "second volume" of Luke-Acts), we need to ask how events in the last third of the first century affected the attitudes reflected in documents written during that period.

By the era of the gospels, tensions that existed within and between different early Christian communities had become more pronounced. Whereas Paul, writing in the fifties and early sixties of the first century, had dealt with relations between gentiles and Jews within the church, the gospels reflect a time when some churches had become exclusively gentile communities. These churches existed in some conflict with both the older, Jewish-Christian churches, and also with the synagogues. The gospels were written as pastorally engaged tracts, intended to support the new gentile communities in this season of considerable difficulty and crisis.

A Period of Transition: The Gospel of Mark

When the Gospel of Mark was written, the church was undergoing a passage from its initial home in Jerusalem and in Judaism to the gentile civilization of the Roman Empire. The older church was composed of Peter and the other original apostles of Jesus and some of Jesus' family members, such as James, his brother.

Members of this church and others like it are often referred to as "Jewish-Christians," a not particularly helpful name. The earliest record of Jesus' followers' calling themselves "Christians" is 1 Peter 4:16, a book probably written during the persecutions under the emperor Trajan, who reigned in the years 98-117 (Perrin: 257). Earlier Christians apparently referred to themselves as "belonging to the Way." Also, all early followers of Jesus would have been "Jewish-Christians." That is, both Paul and Peter, who disagreed with each other, were Jews who decided to follow Jesus. The term "Jewish-Christians" blurs their differences. Because the intent of the term "Jewish-Christians" is to point to those followers of Jesus who adhered to the beliefs and practices of the earliest church, we will call them "conservative followers of Jesus."

The conservative followers of Jesus held firmly to traditional Jewish customs, including circumcision and the food laws, whereas the more recent gentile churches saw no reason to observe these practices. More importantly, the conservatives primarily thought of Jesus under the concept of the Messiah, whereas the newer gentile communities thought of him in characteristic gentile ways as a divine being, the son of God, or Lord.

That strain could well arise between innovative and conservative members of the same religious group is no surprise. All such transitions are characterized by tension between those introducing new ways of belief and practice (the liberals) and those who defend inherited forms of belief and practice (the conservatives). Because the conservatives, the Jerusalem church of the apostles and Jesus' family, took the twelve apostles as their authorities, Mark goes out of his way to show that the original apostles and Jesus' family fail to be trustworthy guides to the religious life by making it "plain to the reader that the Twelve never understood Jesus properly" (Pherigo: 644).

Consequently, the theme of conflict dominates Mark's gospel, conflict between Jesus and his family, his disciples, and six different groups of "official" Jews. Unless Christian preachers and teachers are alert to what is going on, they may fall into the trap of teaching that Jesus' life was lived and his gospel preached in antagonism to everything Jewish. What really happened is that Mark read back into the career of Jesus the conflicts that he and his community underwent in the late first century. "Enemies of the church are depicted as enemies of Jesus," says Paul Winter, who concludes: "All the Marcan 'controversy stories,' without exception, reflect disputes between the 'Apostolic Church' and its social environment, and are devoid of circumstances in the life of Jesus" (Winter: 120, 125).

In working with Mark, we need to be alert to the sheer volume of conflict present in it. First, the *family* of Jesus, associated with Mark's conservative opponents, think Jesus is out of his mind (3:19-22), and he rebuffs them (3:31-15). Second, Mark claims that the *twelve apostles*, authoritative for the conservatives, failed to understand the feeding of the five thousand because of their hardened hearts (6:51-52), missed the point of a parable and were asked by Jesus, "Are you also without understanding?" (7:18), and again missed the point after the feeding of the four thousand, only to have Jesus ask them: "Do you not yet perceive or understand? Are your hearts hardened?" (8:17).

Third, *Peter*, chief among the apostles, was rebuked by Jesus immediately after confessing "You are the Christ" (8:29) with the saying: "Get behind me, Satan! For you are not on the side of God, but of men" (8:33). The disciples are a "faithless generation"

(9:19) and again fail to understand Jesus (9:32). At the end, three times the disciples fail to stay awake with Jesus prior to his arrest (14:32-42). Judas betrays him (14:43-50), and Peter denies Jesus three times (14:66-72). Even the three women, Mary Magdalene, Mary the mother of James, and Salome, who found the tomb empty and heard the announcement of the resurrection, "said nothing to any one, for they were afraid" (16:8).

In other words, Mark did a radically new thing: He invented the written gospel, a new kind of literature. He wrote it for an emerging gentile community unsure of its legitimacy in the face of criticism from the older, conservative tradition, an *oral* tradition. Mark claims that all the bearers of this oral tradition—Jesus' family, his apostles, and the women in the community—failed. They did not understand Jesus, hardened their hearts against him, failed him at Gethsemane, betrayed and denied him, did not witness the trial and crucifixion, and having seen the empty tomb and heard of the resurrection, told no one.

Mark also undermines the authority of the conservative followers of Jesus by giving negative roles to six different groups of "official" Jews. The Pharisees are mentioned twelve times, always in conflict with Jesus, usually over such issues as observing the Sabbath (2:27), eating without a ritual washing of the hands (7:1-8), the food laws (the *kosher* or *kashrut* system) (7:15-23), and questions on divorce (10:1-9) and taxes (12:13-17). In rejecting Pharisaic teaching on these matters, Mark's Jesus is made to reject the practices of conservative followers of Jesus of Mark's own time. Also, murderous intentions are attributed to the Pharisees early in the gospel (3:6).

Other groups of official Jews—scribes, Herodians, elders, chief priests, and the Sanhedrin—fare no better. In all, these six groups appear a total of fifty-six times in the fifteen chapters of Mark's short gospel. Each time they appear, the occasion is one of hostility, and the mounting tension results in Jesus' crucifixion. As Jesus expires on the cross, a Roman centurion (note: a gentile) says: "Truly this man was the Son of God" (15:39). Whereas the apostles never understood, a gentile confesses. Mark's pattern seems to be that Jews reject Jesus and the apostles fail him, the result being that the gospel goes to the gentiles. The centurion's confession is the christological climax of Mark, and it takes place while the original Jewish apostles fail to be present.

Mark and the Teaching of Respect

In order to teach and preach from Mark and not engage in the teaching of contempt for Jews and Judaism, we need to remember a few points. First, the gospel—the promise of the love of God for each and all, and therefore the command of God that justice be done to each and all—is at the heart of Mark. Mark dramatically has Jesus announce this gospel at the very beginning of the story (1:4). All our teaching must conform to the gospel, which is the heart of the matter for Mark as it is for all Christians. Never may we deny God's love for Jews nor may we fail to do justice to them.

Second, we need to realize that Mark's purpose was to communicate to a small and beleaguered community, a community that was radically alienated from all surrounding groups and that could expect little except suspicion and hostility, that God loved them (Kee: 100). Mark's message was intended to encourage and support this community, to assure it of God's care. We need to communicate this same message to our own communities, while learning, at the same time, not to deny God's love for all others. Whatever Mark's intention, his way of telling the story of Jesus can be interpreted or, rather, misinterpreted, to say that God has given up on Jews. Particularly, his parable of the vineyard whose tenants will be kicked out and replaced by new tenants (12:1-12), can be read in just this way. We should not read it that way but as a statement of the seriousness of God's purposes for human beings and of our tendency to disappoint God. Instead of treating it as a statement rejecting *them*, we should read it as a prophetic criticism of *us*. Prophetic criticism is always self-criticism before it is criticism of others; we may never turn it into an uncritical rejection of others.

Third, we need to remember that Mark had no interest whatever in relating accurately what happened between Jesus and other Jews. It is fallacious "to think that the statements expressed or implied in the narrative of Mark are a 'direct' representation of the events of Jesus' day" (Rhoads: 413). Nasty images of Jews appear in Mark in the service of Mark's purpose of supporting his community in its conflict with conservative Christians and with the synagogue of Mark's time (13:9). If all the images of Jews that are highlighted in church are negative, congregations will tend to hold such images of their Jewish neighbors. Hence, the church will continue to spread the teaching of contempt. Therefore, we must clarify what was going on in Mark and help people see how Mark must be understood. We must be willing to speak against the text, when failing to do so allows prejudice to continue to do its destructive work.

Of course, these three points—that we are to interpret texts in the light of God's love for and command that justice be done to each and all, that we are to engage in prophetic self-criticism and not to use texts to justify the notion that God has rejected whole peoples, and that we sometimes have to speak critically of texts in the light of deeper insights within the texts themselves—apply not only to Mark but to all biblical texts.

Matthew and the Teaching of Respect

Having dealt as fully as we have with Mark, we can treat Matthew more briefly by pointing out how he differs from Mark and how his treatment of Jews diverges from what we found in Mark. Matthew's gospel was written subsequent to Mark and is concerned with the calling of the church to "make disciples of all nations" (28:19), yet it "tends to focus more sharply on the mission of the church to the Jews" (Perrin: 169). As Matthew gave form to his understanding of the gospel, he was conversant with what was happening in Judaism in his own time. At this time, which was after the war with Rome that resulted in the destruction of the Temple, the Pharisees emerged as the group that took the lead in rebuilding Jewish faith from the ashes of war. They moved to the coastal town of Jamnia (Javneh) and set up a center where they began to "codify the interpretation of the Law, and in general to systematize matters of belief and practice" (Perrin: 170). Judaism as we know it today stems from this beginning.

Matthew wrote for a church that was closely related to, if separated from, the synagogue across the street (Stendahl: 1968: xi). This synagogue looked to the Pharisees of its day for leadership. Matthew obviously respects what the Pharisees taught, as we can see from a quick look at certain features of his gospel. He patterns Jesus' life and teachings on the model of Moses. Like Moses, Jesus almost died in infancy (2:16-18), was in Egypt for a while (2:13-15), and was called to come out of it (2:15).

As Moses brought the *Torah* down from Mount Sinai, so Jesus presents a sermon on the mount (5:1—7:29). As Moses' teachings are presented in five books, so Jesus' teachings are set forth in five large blocks of sayings, each ending with a definite termination: "And when Jesus had finished these sayings . . ." (7:28). Matthew presents Jesus as "a lawgiver surpassing Moses" who provided a law more demanding than that of Moses (Sandmel: 353). Also, the familiar method by which Jesus taught in Matthew was to comment on and modify the tradition: "You have heard it said . . . , but I say unto you . . . ." This is similar to the Pharisaic practice of "oral *Torah*": "It is written . . . , but the meaning is . . . ."

Matthew changes the picture of Jesus' relations to the Pharisees. Jesus admits that the Pharisees are the proper interpreters of the *Torah* and says that they must be listened to, but he charges them with lack of personal integrity (Sandmel: 354). Matthew 23 is a long diatribe, in which Matthew would have us believe that Jesus made a relentless and hostile attack upon the scribes and Pharisees. In this chapter he calls them "hypocrites" seven times. Yet at the beginning of this diatribe, he says: "The scribes and Pharisees sit on Moses' seat; so practice and observe whatever they tell you, but not what they do; for they preach, but do not practice" (23:1-3).

How do we preach or teach from Matthew and yet teach respect for Jews and Judaism, particularly since we have just seen that the form of Judaism that we now know arose from the activity of these very Pharisees whom Matthew constantly accuses of a lack of personal integrity? First, by remembering the three points made at the end of the discussion of Mark; there is no need to repeat them here. Second, by noting that the conflicts between Jesus and the Pharisees in Matthew tell us more about Matthew's relation to Pharisees than about Jesus: "So the diatribe against 'the scribes and Pharisees' in Matthew 23 does not reflect a conflict between Jesus and the scribes and Pharisees of his day, but one fifty years later between Matthew and their descendants spreading their influence from Jamnia" (Perrin: 171).

Third, we should notice a most important point: When Matthew injects this kind of personal assault against certain Jews into a saying of Jesus, he introduces something ugly into an otherwise beautiful saying. Also, the introduction of this ugly feature contradicts the teaching of Jesus that Matthew relates. What we should do is to excise the ugly attack from the teaching, because the teaching demands it. The following example illustrates this point.

In the Sermon on the Mount, Matthew relates Jesus' saying, "Judge not, that you be not judged" (7:1). This is followed by the saying about seeing the speck in the brother's eye and not noticing the log in one's own eye. Then the bomb is dropped: "You hypocrite" (7:5). By inserting this bit of name-calling into the text, Matthew renders it contradictory. The message seems to be: "Judge not, you hypocrite!" or: "Quit name-calling, jerk!" The text is made to commit the sin against which it preaches.

How should a Christian preacher handle this? First, by noting the result (compromising the teaching that is offered) of Matthew's editing of a piece of name-calling into the text. Second, by observing that Matthew had a fondness for calling people "hypocrites." Of the eighteen occurrences of "hypocrite" in the New Testament, fourteen are in Matthew. Third, by noting that only Jews get called "hypocrites" in Matthew. From Matthew more than any other source, Christians continue to derive the idea that Jews are essentially hypocritical. Jews serve the purposes of Christian polemic by symbolizing everything bad in religion. Fourth, by remarking that this deprives us of the right to be hypocrites. Is hypocrisy a sin that only Jews can commit? Am I not sometimes guilty of it?

When we learn about the Judaism of Jesus' time, we discover that this very commandment against being judgmental toward our neighbors is one we took over from Judaism. Hillel, an older contemporary of Jesus and leader of the "liberal" Pharisaic school, is attributed by the *Mishnah* with the saying: "Judge not thy fellowman until you are come into his place." Other rabbis made similar remarks. The other saying in Matthew 7, about taking the log out of one's own eye before removing the speck from the neighbor's, was a popular Jewish folk saying about people who are unwilling to accept criticism or who are quick to notice in others the faults that they also have but are unwilling to recognize in themselves. This is not to suggest that Matthew's quotation does not come from Jesus, but it is to suggest that many sayings attributed to Jesus are closely parallel to Pharisaic sayings, some of which are attributed to Hillel.

The text from Matthew, which preaches against being judgmental, is itself judgmental toward Jews. If we are to learn from it, we must learn not to be judgmental toward all our neighbors, Jews included. By his more basic teaching we are freed to deal critically with Matthew's judgmental attitudes.

Luke-Acts and the Teaching of Respect

The Gospel According to Luke and the Acts of the Apostles are two volumes of one work, intended to be read together. When the church put together the canon of the New Testament in the fourth century, the two were separated by the Gospel of John. Luke addressed each book to "most excellent Theophilus" (Luke 1:1-4; Acts 1:1-2), and was concerned "to help the church normalize its relations with the Roman Empire and its members settle down to Christian witness in a continuing world" (Perrin: 197). Telltale clues are the way Luke's story is consistently related to the Roman Empire. Joseph and Mary went to Bethlehem "when Quirinius was governor of Syria" in response to a decree from Caesar Augustus (Luke 2:1-2). The preaching career of John the Baptizer began "in the fifteenth year of the reign of Tiberius Caesar, Pontius Pilate being governor of Judea, and Herod being tetrarch of Galilee, and his brother Philip tetrarch of the region of Ituraea and Trachonitis, and Lysanius tetrarch of Abilene" (Luke 3:1).

Luke reconstructs history to make Roman officials innocent of persecuting Christians and to lay all the blame for the difficulties that Christians had on Jews. Whereas Mark and Matthew relate that Herod, a Roman Tetrarch, beheaded John the Baptizer (Mark 6:16; Matthew 14:10), Luke merely comments that Herod "shut up John in prison" (Luke 3:20). Pilate is completely innocent of the crucifixion of Jesus, and three times asks: "What evil has he done?" (Luke 23:1-25). Officials of the Roman Empire find Paul innocent of charges brought against him by "the Jews": "This man is doing nothing to deserve death or imprisonment" (Acts 26:31). Whereas the Christian tradition notes that Paul (and Peter) died in Rome because of Nero's persecution of Christians, Acts ends by saying that Paul "lived there two whole years at his own expense, and welcomed all who came to him, preaching the kingdom of God and teaching about the Lord Jesus Christ quite openly and unhindered" (Acts 28:30). It is silent about Nero's execution of Christians.

Meanwhile, Christians, like Jesus before them, are continually bushwhacked by the Jews, who are consistently malevolent in Luke's writing. In Acts, the expression "the Jews" occurs forty-nine times, and "Jews" fifteen times. In Luke "all those in the synagogue" try to kill Jesus at the outset of his ministry (4:28-29), scribes and Pharisees are "filled with fury" against Jesus (6:11), and the pattern continues throughout Luke-Acts. The verbal shift in Acts is away from naming specific Jewish groups to saying "the Jews." "The Jews" revile Paul (Acts 13:45). "The Jews" stir up persecution against Paul and Barnabas (13:50). "The Jews" poison the minds of gentiles against the church (14:2). "The Jews" engineer a mob action against Paul and Silas (17:5). "The Jews" incite the crowds against Paul at Beroea (17:13). "The Jews" bring Paul before the tribunal (18:12). "The Jews" stir up a crowd in Jerusalem against Paul (21:27). "The Jews" swear to kill Paul (23:12). "The Jews" lie in ambush for Paul (23:21). "The Jews" join in a charge against Paul (24:9). "The Jews" file many false charges against Paul (25:7).

In contrast to what Acts says about Paul's difficulties. Paul himself indicates that while he indeed had troubles, they arose from many sources: "in danger from rivers, danger from robbers, danger from my own people, danger from Gentiles, danger in the city, danger in the wilderness, danger at sea, danger from false brethren" (2 Corinthians 11:26). Whereas Acts singles out "the Jews" as Paul's source of trouble, Paul indicates that his difficulties had many sources, the chief of which was not Jews but his fellow Christians. The conclusion is that these passages about "the Jews" "represent an anti-Jewish reconstruction of history" (Slingerland: 318). They are nothing more than a series of vilifications of Jews, apparently intended to demonstrate that whatever was of value in the old legal religion of Judaism has now passed into the church (Slingerland: 319).

"The Jews" fare no better in the speeches given in Luke-Acts than they do in the narrative. In them, the Jews are accused of having committed a trail of crimes. Peter's sermon charges: "this Jesus . . . you crucified and killed by the hand of lawless men" (Acts 2:23); "God has made him both Lord and Christ, this Jesus whom you crucified" (Acts 2:36). Stephen taxes them with having murdered the Righteous One, as their fathers killed the prophets (Acts 7:51-53). This is finger-pointing, accusational religion; it does not confess sin, it indicts. It is not "I have sinned," but "you have sinned." All this "represents more a theological tendency than any historical tradition" (Jack T. Sanders: 19).

Luke's final view is two-fold: First, Jews never understand the gospel (Luke 2:50; 8:10; 9:45; Acts 7:25; 13:27) and never will (Acts 28:26). Consequently, it goes to the gentiles: "Let it be known to you then that this salvation of God has been sent to the Gentiles; they will listen" (Acts 28:28). Second, Jews deserve only to be slaughtered for their lack of faith and their hostility. Luke has Jesus say: "But as for these enemies of mine, who did not want me to reign over them, bring them here and slay them before me" (Luke 19:27). To Paul, Luke attributes the remark: "Your blood be upon your heads!" (Acts 18:6). Luke's two books obviously contain the leaven of anti-Judaism "against which we must all eternally be on guard" (Jack T. Sanders: 317).

How do we manage to teach respect for Jews and Judaism when dealing with passages from Luke-Acts, particularly those characterized by the kind of bias we have seen? First, we have to remember the points made about Mark and Matthew; they apply here as well. Second, we have to remember that what we are to proclaim is the gospel, the good news of God's love graciously offered to each and all and the command of God that justice be done to each and all of those whom God loves. Luke-Acts can be read as the extension of the light to gentiles, without continuing to assume that the gospel can go to gentiles (us) only at the expense of Jews. Indeed, in some places Luke-Acts itself seems to realize this, as when it tells of Jesus' presentation as an infant in the temple. Quoting Isaiah, Simeon refers to Jesus as "a light for revelation to the Gentiles, and for glory to thy people Israel" (Luke 2:32). Sadly, most of Luke-Acts strips Israel of its glory. Nonetheless, the story should be reinterpreted in the light of this quotation from Isaiah.

Third, the preacher should note a certain problem with the parables of Jesus as Luke has edited them. This problem occurs also in other gospels. As they stand, the parables can be read as if "Jews—observant Jews—were the losers and gentiles were the winners" (Sloyan: 91). The gospel writers "surely added a church vs. non-church bite to Jesus' parables" (Sloyan: 92). For example,

Luke's famous parable of the good Samaritan can be readily misinterpreted (Luke 10:29-37). The two characters who do not respond to the injured victim on the roadside are a priest and a Levite, both Jews. But a foreigner does works of love and mercy. If the unexpected twist of the parable is in saying that goodness occurs where it is least expected, perhaps it should be retold as the parable of the good Jew. The likelihood is great that Luke edited his Samaritan into the parable because it fits his obvious theological perspective that the gospel goes *from* the Jews, *through* the periphery (Samaritans, outcasts), *to* gentiles. We have seen the dangers of that perspective.

The story of the ten lepers who were cleansed (Luke 17:11-19) is an example of how Luke's editing of a Samaritan into the story makes for an awkward result. Alone among the ten lepers healed, one (a Samaritan) returns to thank Jesus. The Jewish lepers do not. In the story both Jesus and the lepers conduct themselves according to the *Torah* regulations for lepers. Jesus' sending them to the temple followed the Levitical procedure for the readmission of lepers to normal society (Leviticus 13). The nine Jewish lepers who do what Jesus commanded them to do are criticized for having done so. The Samaritan is said to be the only one who gives praise to God, yet that is exactly what the Jewish lepers would have done in the temple. The Samaritan is said to have been healed by his faith. What healed the Jewish lepers? Preachers working with this story should grasp the basic point that it is God who is the nurturing and healing ground of the life of all people; the story should be interpreted theocentrically. Doing so will correlate it with the earlier story in Luke of the rich man and Lazarus (16:19-31), the main point of which is that "Moses and the prophets" speak a sufficient call to repentance.

John and the Teaching of Respect

John is no doubt the most extreme of the gospels in setting up a contrast between Christians and Jews (Brown, 1966: lxx). He uses the term "the Jews" over sixty times, whereas it appears only fifteen times in the first three gospels taken together. Late in the first century, many Jewish groups had disappeared, Judaism became more homogeneous, and John speaks of "the Jews" of his day. They symbolize what is old, temporal, outward, and carnal, in contrast to the new, eternal, inward, and spiritual church.

> "The Jews" are programmatically identified with this false principle of existence of the world of darkness here below. John's midrash works constantly between the eternal, spiritual meaning of every symbol and its carnal, inauthentic mode of appropriation in Judaism (Reuther: 111).

John's Jesus speaks to Jews as if he were not one of them (7:19; 8:17; 10:34). "They hated me without a cause," he says (15:25; 19:27). "Their law" has been superseded because the scriptures point to Christ: "I am the way, and the truth, and the life; no one comes to the Father, but by me" (14:6). Jews who do not convert to the church are blind and miss salvation: "You search the scriptures, because you think that in them you have eternal life; and it is they who bear witness to me; yet you refuse to come to me that you may have life" (5:39-40). Jews do not know Jesus and do not know God (7:28; 8:19). The reason that they do not hear is that they "are not of God" (8:47). Rather, their father is the devil (8:44), a murderer and a liar, and the will of "the Jews" is to do their father's wishes (8:44).

All of this nasty talk about Jews occurs in a gospel that also has positive things to say about Jews, one of the more striking of which is Jesus' comment: "salvation is from the Jews" (4:22). The resulting contradiction that John contains both anti-Jewish and relatively pro-Jewish elements needs an explanation. The scholarly consensus is that the community that produced the fourth gospel was initially a Jewish-Christian group that later was expelled from the synagogues (Brown, 1979: 22). Apparently the expulsion took place after the Pharisaic academy at Jamnia changed the liturgy to make it impossible for Christians to participate (Perrin: 230). The earlier layer of John's gospel contains traditional material that circulated in this Jewish-Christian community; the later layer has been edited in an anti-Jewish direction (Townsend: 81-84).

John's community was obviously angered and anguished by this ejection from the synagogue. They deeply desired to be *Jewish*-Christians and responded as people do in a family fight, which is the most bitter kind of brawl. John's gospel reflects the animosity of one side in the conflict. "The smoldering feud had led to a separation" (Cope: 31).

How are we to deal with John's gospel? First, we have to agree with theologian David Tracy when he says that the "anti-Judaic statements of the New Testament bear *no* authoritative status for Christianity . . . . The heart of the New Testament message—the love who is God—should release the demythologizing power of its own prophetic meaning to rid the New Testament and Christianity once and for all of these statements" (Tracy: 94). Understanding how these statements came into John enables us to relativize them.

Second, we note that in John we find some of the most profound statements about the Christian life: "A new commandment I give to you, that you love one another; even as I have loved you, that you also love one another. By this all men will know that you are my disciples, if you have love for one another" (13:34-35). This new commandment, by the way, is a "renewed" (*kainos*) commandment, not a brand new one. We cannot keep it and at the same time retain John's nasty attitude toward Jews.

Third, in contrast to his exclusivism, John sometimes takes a different view: "I have other sheep, that are not of this fold" (10:16). God indeed has sheep of whom we know not.

Conclusion

In this chapter, we have dealt with the texts in the New Testament that regularly give Christians the greatest difficulty when we seek to make the Christian witness without spreading prejudice against our Jewish neighbors. The gospels were all redacted (edited, but creatively and not in a scissors-and-paste manner) in the late first century, at a time of great tension and hostility. The conflicts in which the young church found itself were both internal and external.

The internal conflicts were between different kinds of Christians, of which there were several. John's gospel, for example, is opposed not only to Jews, but to other kinds of Christians who have too low a christology (Brown, 1979: 43ff.). John would have disdained the christologies of Mark, Matthew, and Luke. External conflicts were also with more than one group. The gospels frequently indicate tension with and persecution from synagogues.

While we may question how intensive this really was, there was obviously something to it. Paul regrets having persecuted the churches prior to his call (Galatians 1:13). Also, there was the obvious conflict with Rome, beginning at least as early as Nero's execution of Christians in the year 64.

The gospels were written as tracts for the times and should be looked upon as emergency literature. They addressed the needs of minority, threatened communities surrounded by alienation and suspicion. Early Christians were better Jews than they knew, and very poor pagans. They did not fit in well in the religious society of their day.

Biblical writers usually made use of one or the other of two strategies. To a community that needed comfort (Latin: *com* + *fort* = "with strength"), strengthening, they would say, "God loves *you*, perhaps *only* you." "You only have I known of all the families of the earth" (Amos 3:2) is one way God can speak to Israel. We will call this the "edifying" form of biblical speech. To a community that in its complacency needed challenging, they would point out that God loves *all* the children of the earth, and that justice must be done to them. You shall love the stranger, the foreigner, as yourself (Leviticus 19:34). We shall call this the "prophetic" way of talking.

To teach the Bible only in the light of the edifying interpretation is to communicate to our congregations that God loves us but nobody else. Sometimes this takes denominational form: God loves only members of our denomination. The edifying interpretation, without the prophetic, is idolatrous. To teach the Bible only in the light of the prophetic approach is to say that God loves everybody else but not us. This challenges but does not comfort, whereas the former comforts without challenging. The edifying approach alone is idolatrous, and the prophetic approach alone is empty.

How can Christians preach a firm word of hope and do it while respecting others? The answer is easy: Keep the edifying and prophetic modes of biblical speech linked firmly together.

4

A Witness People—Jews in a Christian Context

Introduction

From the victory of Rome over Jewish forces in 135 C.E. until the founding of the state of Israel in 1948, Jews lived in lands controlled by others. The terms of their existence were set by what the larger society permitted Jews to do. Although Jews lived in many societies—Roman, Muslim, Russian—we will concentrate on how they were treated in a Christian context and on how this treatment contributed to the making of the Nazi era. Along this historical course, we will note the images of Jews and Judaism in Christian history and the survival of these images in new forms in the present.

Christian Images of Jews

Judaism got off to a new beginning at Jamnia under the leadership of the rabbis who recreated Judaism after the fall of the temple in 70 C.E. Until the early fifth century, Judaism and Christianity grew up together in the Roman Empire. In this context, Jews fared well. Their condition was indistinguishable from that of other peoples, and they were exempted from worshiping the emperor (Roth:138). They were the object of literary ridicule from the Roman writers (as were Christians). Yet large numbers of people became "God-fearers," listening in at the synagogue and adhering to certain Jewish observances, such as resting on the Sabbath.

In ordinary life under the Roman Empire, Jews were free.

They could engage in any business or cultural activity. As a result of the Edict of Caracalla, issued by the emperor Marcus Aurelius in 212 C.E., Roman citizenship was extended to all free residents of the Empire. The purpose was to make more people pay taxes, but for Jews it meant that they were citizens in every respect. This situation continued until the first Christian emperor, Constantine (emperor from 324 to 337 C.E.), when the position of Jews began to deteriorate. Until the early fourth century, Christian images of Jews were expressed verbally. Beginning then, these images were incorporated into the social fabric of everyday life.

Jews in Christian Rhetoric

We will look at the major images of Jews and Judaism that shaped how Christians thought of Jews. These images played an important role in Christian communities. They helped to form a sense of Christian social identity, to tell Christians who they were by telling them who they were not. Christians were given to understand that they were not Jewish, that they were anti-Jewish, and that they were better than Jewish. Jews became the foil over against whom Christians defined themselves. Also clear in the literature is the fact that relationships between Jews and Christians were often quite cordial. Indeed, it is just this against which many Christian preachers complained.

Jews are *a rejected people*. In the *Letter of Barnabas* probably written for a gentile community in Alexandria, Egypt, in the early second century, the writer takes offense at the views of some members of the church. They recklessly say that the covenant belongs both to Jews and to the church (Barnabas: 145). To oppose this teaching, Barnabas explains that the covenant between God and the Jews has been "abolished" and replaced by a new one with a new people—us. We are the ones whom God has led into the land of promise (Barnabas: 141). The "Old" Testament deals entirely with shadows, whereas the light of reality shines in the New. All Jewish observance, relying as it does on the covenant that has been annulled, is illegitimate. Jews have "proved themselves unworthy" and have been displaced by us (Barnabas: 146-147). Religiously, Jews are out of business; if they would only see the light, they would convert to Christianity and cease to exist as Jews.

Jews are *a deicide people*. In Sardis, an ancient city in west Asia Minor (Turkey), a bishop named Melito (who died ca. 190 C.E.) preached a sermon "On the Passover." He contrasted the "old" type with the "new" reality, arguing that the type, to which Jews adhere, was "discarded" when the reality arrived. A dressmaker starts with a pattern, discarding it when the dress is finished, "so also the law was finished when the gospel was revealed, and the people was abandoned when the church was established" (Melito: 29). To this view Melito added the charge of killing God:

> He who hung the earth was hung;
> he who affixed the heavens was affixed;
> he who sustained all was suspended on the tree;
> the master has been outraged;
> God has been murdered;
> the King of Israel slain by Israelite hand
> (Melito: 47).

Melito's charge of killing God would become a staple ingredient of popular Christian consciousness.

Jews are *a blind people*. Justin Martyr, an apologist for Christianity, lived in the second century (ca. 100-165) in Rome. Although all the themes of anti-Judaism are present in his works, the one that stands out is that of Jewish blindness to the gospel. Regarding Jewish study of the scriptures, Justin said: "They, though they read, do not understand what is said" (Justin: 173). Jews are guilty of not recognizing the Messiah; and when he appeared, they killed him. "Not knowing this One, the Logos, Jews failed to know God" (Justin: 184). Because of their blindness and hardness of heart, Jews despise and slight the new covenant. In spite of the presence of the lawgiver, Jews do not see him; even when the blind see, Jews fail to understand (Justin: 201). Accordingly, Jews suffer deservedly from the lack of a homeland (Rome expelled Jews from Jerusalem after the war in 135 C.E.).

Jews are *an apostate people*. In his anti-Jewish tract, *An Answer to the Jews*, Tertullian (ca. 160-225), a north African theologian, charged Jews with having deserted God by failing to convert to Christianity. Whereas the gentiles had departed from idolatry to worship God, Jews "quite forsook God" in not departing from faith in the God of Israel (Tertullian: 152). Therefore the ills that befall Jews in being banished from Jerusalem are simply their due (Tertullian: 174). Tertullian regarded the suffering of Jews in his day as verifying the remark in Matthew: "His blood be upon us and upon our children" (Tertullian: 160).

Jews are *a people without rights*. Ambrose (ca. 339-397) was bishop of Milan and one of the four "doctors" (teachers) of the church. In 388 C.E., some Christians, at the urging of their bishop, burned a synagogue in the town of Callinicum on the Euphrates river. The emperor Theodosius, learning of this crime, ordered the bishop to rebuild the synagogue and punish those who destroyed it.

When Ambrose learned of this order, he argued that a synagogue could not be rebuilt with Christian money and threatened to excommunicate Theodosius. In a letter to his sister, Ambrose describes the sermon he preached when Theodosius was next in church. Ambrose asserts that bishops have a right to burn synagogues "that there may be no place in which Christ is denied" (Ambrose: 232). He contends that because the synagogue is no more than "a place of unbelief, a home of impiety, a refuge of insanity, damned by God himself," we should not be disturbed by its being burnt (Ambrose: 234). He uses his anti-Jewish ideology to justify criminal actions against Jews and to permit Christians to attack Jewish property with impunity.

Jews are *a wandering people*. In the fifth century, Augustine (ca. 354-430) created the myth of the "wandering Jew," the people who, because of their unbelief, are condemned to wander the earth. In their homelessness they provide what he called "a strange witness of unbelief." Augustine developed his view in an allegory on the Cain and Abel story (Genesis 4:1-16).

As Cain slew Abel, so the Jews killed Christ. As Abel was innocent, so is Christ. As Cain is cursed to be a mourner, so the Jews are cursed from the church. The Jews are to suffer for their crime, but we are not to make them suffer. Their destiny is to "wander" the earth, testifying to the fate of those who reject Christ. To the end of time, the Jews are to be preserved in this abject condition (Augustine: 28-32).

The practice of the church was, consequently, twofold: to protect Jews, so that they could make their witness, and to define